GALE
CENGAGE Learning

Drama for Students, Volume 15

Project Editor: David Galens

Editorial: Anne Marie Hacht, Michelle Kazensky, Michael L. LaBlanc, Ira Mark Milne, Pam Revitzer, Jennifer Smith, Daniel Toronto, Carol Ullmann
Permissions: Kim Davis, Debra Freitas

Manufacturing: Stacy Melson

Imaging and Multimedia: Lezlie Light, Kelly A. Quin, Luke Rademacher **Product Design**: Pamela A. E. Galbreath, Michael Logusz © 2002 by Gale. Gale is an imprint of The Gale Group, Inc., a division of Cengage Learning Inc.

Gale and Design™ and Cengage Learning™ are trademarks used herein under license.

For more information, contact
The Gale Group, Inc.
27500 Drake Rd.
Farmington Hills, Ml 48331-3535

Or you can visit our Internet site at
http://www.gale.com

ALL RIGHTS RESERVED

service, or individual does not imply endorsement of the editors or publisher. Errors brought to the attention of the publisher and verified to the satisfaction of the publisher will be corrected in future editions.

ISBN 0-7876-5253-9
ISSN 1094-9232

Printed in the United States of America
10 9 8 7 6 5 4 3

J. B.

Archibald Macleish 1958

Introduction

J. B., published in 1958, is a play in verse based on the biblical story of Job. It represents Archibald MacLeish's responses to the horrors he saw during two world wars, including the Holocaust and the bombings of Hiroshima and Nagasaki. The author explains in the foreword to the acting edition of his play that turning to the Bible for a framework seems sensible "when you are dealing with questions too large for you which, nevertheless, will not leave you alone." *J. B.* tells the story of a twentieth-century American banker-millionaire whom God commands be stripped of his family and his wealth but who refuses to turn his back on God. MacLeish wondered how modern people could retain hope and keep on living with all the suffering in the world and offered this play as an answer. J. B. learns that there is no justice in the world, that happiness and suffering are not deserved, and that people can still choose to love each other and live.

MacLeish had been earning his living as a poet for fifty years before this, his third verse play, was published. Shortly after the publication of the book, the play was produced on Broadway and underwent substantial revisions. There are, therefore, two versions of the play available for readers: the original book published by Houghton Mifflin and the acting script available from Samuel French. Both were published in 1958, and neither has ever gone out of print. *J. B.* won the Pulitzer Prize for drama in 1959 (MacLeish's third Pulitzer), as well as the Tony Award for best play. More important, the play sparked a national conversation about the nature of God, the nature of hope, and the role of the artist in society.

Author Biography

Archibald MacLeish was born in Glencoe, Illinois, on May 7, 1892. His father was a successful businessman, and his mother had been a college instructor; they saw to it that MacLeish was well educated. He attended public schools in Glencoe, and at the age of fifteen he was sent to a college preparatory academy in Connecticut. He began college studies at Yale in 1911.

Before college, MacLeish had been only an average student. At Yale, however, he began writing poetry and fiction for the literary magazine, excelled in water polo and football, earned high grades, and was elected to the Phi Beta Kappa honorary society. After graduation in 1915, he entered Harvard Law School, hoping that a career in law would give him a way to bring order out of chaos, just as poetry did. He married Ada Hitchcock in 1916; served briefly in the army; published his first book of poetry, *Tower of Ivory,* in 1917; and graduated first in his law school class in 1919. He taught government at Harvard for a short time and then worked as an attorney in Boston, but never lost his devotion to writing poetry.

In 1923, MacLeish moved with his family to Paris, determined to become a serious poet. During this period, many important American and European writers were living in Paris, and MacLeish became friendly with them, determined to learn from them. He taught himself Italian, so he could study the work of the fourteenth-century poet Dante Alighieri, and he studied the history of English poetry as well. These five years transformed his work, giving him a mature style that pleased both him and the critics. When he returned home, he was able to earn a living as a writer and to buy a small farm in Massachusetts where he and Ada lived together until his death.

His will to bring order and harmony to human existence informed MacLeish's career for the next sixty years. He published more than fifty books of poetry, drama, and essays, but he also accepted positions as the Librarian of Congress, Assistant Secretary of State, and part of the U.S. Delegation to the United Nations that established the United Nations Educational, Scientific and Cultural Organization (UNESCO). He believed that the poet's duty was to address contemporary social concerns and to ask important questions. His distress at the bombings of Dresden, London, and Hiroshima led him to wonder how humans could respond with hope to such suffering. He posed this question in the 1958 play, *J. B.*, a retelling of the biblical story of Job, which brought MacLeish several awards and his largest financial success.

Over his career, MacLeish won three Pulitzer Prizes, the National Book Award, a Tony Award, an Academy Award for best screenplay, and nearly two dozen honorary degrees. In 1977, he received the Presidential Medal of Freedom. He died on April 20, 1982, just three weeks before a national symposium honoring his life and work.

Prologue

The first characters to appear on stage in *J. B.* are Mr. Zuss and Nickles, a balloon seller and a popcorn seller in a run-down circus. They approach and then mount a sideshow stage in the corner of a circus tent to play out the story of Job from the Bible, with the stage as Heaven, the ground as Earth, and the lights as the stars. Zuss (whose name sounds like "Zeus," the god of Greek mythology) will play God. From the beginning, he is as arrogant as one might expect a man who believes he is right for the role to be, and he is indignant at the idea that Job would dare to demand justice.

Nickles, on the other hand, understands Job's suffering and does not accept that God would cause that suffering just to prove his authority and power. Nickles sings a song that includes the play's central paradox: "If God is God He is not good,/If God is good, He is not God." Nickles, whose name is a variation of "Old Nick," a slang term for the devil, will play Satan. As the two men point out, there is always someone to play Job.

Zuss and Nickles don masks that they find in a pile of costumes. The Godmask is white, with closed eyes, showing his indifference. The Satanmask is dark, with open eyes, because "Satan sees." They review their lines, which will come from the King James Bible. When the lights go down for the play to begin, a Distant Voice speaks the first line: "Whence comest thou?" It is not Zuss who speaks but, apparently, God. Zuss and Nickels take over, and the lights dim.

Scene 1

As scene 1 begins, the raised stage where Zuss and Nickels stand is in darkness, while gathered around a table in the light are the wealthy banker J. B., his wife Sarah, and their five children. They are a wealthy New England family, celebrating Thanksgiving. Sarah would like the children to be more thankful for the bounty they enjoy. She believes that there is a kind of bargain with God: "If we do our part He does His." Our "part" is to thank God; if we forget God, He will punish. J. B. believes that God has chosen him for success and that his duty is to appreciate the gift, to enjoy his life.

Scene 2

The focus shifts again to Zuss and Nickels, whose first impulse is to belittle J. B.'s acting ability. Still, he is their "pigeon," the man who will play Job. Nickels believes that once J. B. is stripped of his wealth, as Job was, he will lose his piety, but Zuss insists that J. B. will praise God no matter how much he suffers. Why then, asks Nickels, must Job be made to suffer at all? If God knows Job will pass the test, then why administer the test? Because,

Zuss answers, Job needs to see God clearly. The two actors put their masks on and speak lines from the Bible. Satan challenges God to a bet: he will take everything away from Job, to demonstrate that even an upright man will curse God if pushed hard enough. God accepts.

Scene 3

Six or seven years have passed. Two drunken soldiers come to J. B.'s house, comrades in arms of David, J. B.'s oldest son. In a bumbling fashion, they reveal that David has been killed—not heroically in the war but accidentally and stupidly by his own men after the hostilities. As Sarah tries to understand that God has really taken her son, J. B. denies that David is really dead. Nickles encourages them to challenge God, but they do not hear him.

Scene 4

On the sidewalk, two reporters talk to a "Girl," a young woman perhaps in her twenties. They persuade her to approach a couple who will come by soon and to catch their attention so they will be facing the camera when the reporters tell them that two of their children have died in a car accident. The couple, of course, are J. B. and Sarah. The dead teenagers are their children, Mary and Jonathan, killed by a drunk driver when their car crashed into a viaduct. Sarah despairs and asks why God would do this. Nickles, who is visible, grins appreciatively.

But J. B. insists that they cannot "Take the good and not the evil." He tries to embrace Sarah, but she flinches.

Scene 5

J. B. and Sarah talk to two men. The biblical story includes two messengers, and here they are played by police officers. Rebecca, the youngest child, is missing. J. B. did not call the police right away because he imagined that he could find her by himself. Sarah explains bitterly, "We believe in our luck in this house!" The luck again is bad, however. Rebecca has been raped and murdered by a teenaged drug user. "The Lord giveth," J. B. says, "The Lord taketh away." But he does not say the end of the line, which Nickels, Zuss, and the audience are expecting: "Blessed be the name of the Lord."

Scene 6

Two messengers enter carrying Sarah. She has been rescued from a collapsed building after a bombing destroyed a whole city block. J. B.'s bank is destroyed, and his last remaining child, Ruth, is dead. J. B. urges Sarah not to despair, urges her to say with him, "The Lord giveth. The Lord taketh away." While Sarah shouts, "Kills! Kills! Kills! Kills! Kills!" J. B. completes the famous line, "Blessed be the name of the Lord."

Scene 7

Zuss and Nickles discuss J. B. Zuss is pleased with J. B.'s responses so far, but Nickles is disgusted. Although they are playing out a story that both know well, Nickles believes that this time the story will end differently, that J. B. will stop praising God once he experiences physical pain himself. When their argument delays the progress of the story, the Distant Voice begins to speak God's lines. Zuss and Nickles understand that they are to continue.

Scene 8

J. B. lies on a table, clothed only in rags, with Sarah, also in rags, by his side weeping. An atomic blast has killed thousands, and J. B. is wounded. Women standing nearby comment on the sores covering J. B.'s body and on how far the two have fallen. Sarah is bitter and angry, but J. B. is puzzled. He knows there must be a reason for God's punishment, but he cannot fathom what the reason is. Nickles observes that if J. B. knew the reason—if he knew that God was making the innocent J. B. suffer simply to demonstrate His own power—J. B. would despair. Sarah cannot accept J. B.'s theory that the family has deserved this suffering. She turns her back on J. B., urging him to "curse God and die," and she runs out to kill herself. Now completely alone, J. B. begs God to "Show me my guilt." Nickles sneers at Zuss.

Scene 9

In the biblical story, three comforters come to Job to scold him for questioning God and to "justify the ways of God to man." Here, the three comforters are Zophar, a Catholic priest, Eliphaz, a psychiatrist, and Bildad, a Marxist. The three spout empty rhetoric and jargon to explain J. B.'s suffering, and they only add to J. B.'s despair. Finally, J. B. cries out, "God, my God, my God, answer me!" In response, the Distant Voice speaks God's words from the Bible, asserting his power and authority, demanding that J. B./Job repent for daring to ask questions of God. J. B. does, also speaking a line from the Bible, "I abhor myself and repent."

Scene 10

Nickles acknowledges that Zuss has won the bet, but Zuss is uneasy with his victory. He sees that for Job to forgive God is a sign of Job's goodness and strength, not God's. He loses all enthusiasm for playing his role and starts to climb down from the stage, but Nickles reminds him that there is one more scene to play. In the biblical story, God restores everything Job has lost. Nickles is sure that this time J. B./Job will refuse God's offering, that he will not risk losing everything again. To make sure, he goes to J. B., tells him God's plan, and begs him to kill himself instead. But J. B. hears someone at the door and goes to meet his future.

Scene 11

Typically, in a play-within-a-play, the outer play "frames" the other, taking the first and last words. But J. B. and Sarah have the last scene to themselves, without the commentary of Nickles and Zuss. Sarah sits on the doorstep, holding a forsythia branch in bloom. She discovered it on her way to drown herself in the river, found hope in it, and came back to J. B. She explains to her husband, "You wanted justice and there was none—/ Only love." People will not find illumination or love from God, but in their own hearts. Sarah and J. B. embrace and then set to work tidying up the stage.

Characters

Bildad

Bildad is one of the three comforters who come to reassure J. B. in scene 9, after J. B. has lost everything. Spouting jargon-filled cliches, Bildad explains J. B.'s suffering from a Marxist viewpoint, posing an economic answer to J. B.'s problems. J. B. should not wallow in guilt, he claims, because "Guilt is a sociological accident."

David

Thirteen years old at the start of the play, David is the oldest son of J. B. and Sarah. As a young man, David becomes a soldier. He survives the war only to be accidentally killed by his own comrades before he can return home.

Distant Voice

At two points in the play, while Zuss and Nickles are arguing in their roles as God and Satan, another voice from offstage is heard speaking lines attributed to God in the King James Bible. In the list of characters, the voice is named The Distant Voice. As MacLeish himself explained several times, the voice belongs to God himself, another character in the play.

Media Adaptations

- A recording of *J. B.,* performed by some of the actors from the Broadway production, was issued by RCA Victor (LD6075) as a record album around 1960. It has not been reissued on compact disc or audio cassette.

Eliphaz

Eliphaz is one of the three comforters who come to reassure J. B. in scene 9, after J. B. has lost everything. Wearing a white doctor's coat and lecturing like a pompous professor, he speaks for psychiatry, claiming that "Guilt is a / Psychophenomenal situation." His words offer no comfort.

J. B.

J. B. is a perfect and upright man, a successful New England banker, a millionaire, blessed with a loving wife, five children, and a comfortable life. There is no question about his standing for the biblical character Job; his wife Sarah calls him "Job" when she addresses him directly. J. B. is grateful for all he has, but unlike Sarah he does not see the need to express his thanks directly to God; he believes that it is enough to fully appreciate what he has been given. He feels that he is essentially lucky and that all will turn out well in the end. As he suffers each subsequent loss, J. B. insistently thanks God, as Sarah grows increasingly angry. Even after he has lost his family, his wealth, and his physical well-being, J. B. refuses to turn away from God. It is his refusal to "curse God" that finally pushes Sarah to leave him. But J. B.'s optimism is rewarded: God restores everything J. B. has lost and more. The central question of the play comes down to this: knowing he could run the risk of losing them again, how can J. B. accept the new gifts? How can he choose life in a world with no justice?

Jonathan

Jonathan, the younger son of J. B. and Sarah, is three years younger than David. He and his sister Mary are killed by a teenage drunk driver in scene 4.

Mary

Mary is the oldest daughter of J. B. and Sarah. When the play opens, she is twelve years old, a year younger than David. She and her brother Jonathan are killed by a teenage drunk driver in scene 4.

Nickles

Nickles is an old, has-been actor, now reduced to selling popcorn in a derelict circus. As the play begins, he and Mr. Zuss enter the circus tent, find some old masks in a pile of costumes, and take on the roles of God and Satan from the biblical story of Job. Nickles will play Satan (his name is a play on the name "old Nick," a seventeenth-century slang term for the devil) in the play-within-the-play. Nickles's mask is dark, with wide eyes. Unlike Zuss, who plays God, Nickles has some sympathy for Job and bitterness about man's willingness to accept suffering for God's sake. He challenges Zuss to a bet, wagering that if Job were stripped of everything he values, he would curse God. They select J. B. to play Job, and the play-within-the-play begins.

As J. B. loses his children one by one, Nickles/Satan sneers at Zuss/God and his cruel way of showing J. B. his power. Nickles is witty and intelligent, and some critics have said he represents MacLeish in finding humans more worthy of admiration than God. Whereas Zuss is indifferent to J. B.'s suffering, Nickles feels pity. Challenging God and his majesty, Nickles speaks the most frequently quoted lines from the play: "If God is God He is not good, / If God is good He is not God." But when Ruth and twenty thousand others are killed in a bombing and J. B. still praises God, Nickles's feelings turn to disgust. Knowing that at the end of the story God will restore all of J. B.'s treasures, Nickles speaks to J. B. and suggests he kill himself instead. In his last speech, Nickles proclaims violently, "Job won't take it! Job won't touch it!" But he does.

Rebecca

Rebecca, the youngest child of J. B. and Sarah, is only six years old at the beginning of the play. In scene 5 she is raped and murdered by a nineteen-year-old drug user and left in an alley clutching her toy parasol.

Ruth

Ruth, the middle daughter of J. B. and Sarah, is eight years old when the play begins. The last of the children to die, she is killed in the bombing in scene 6 that kills thousands.

Sarah

Sarah is J. B.'s wife of many years and the mother of his five children. Her name is an invention of MacLeish's; Job's wife is not named in the Bible. She is, according to the stage directions, "a fine woman with a laughing, pretty face but a

firm mouth and careful eyes, all New England."
When the family first appears, sharing a
Thanksgiving feast, Sarah insists that they all stop
and thank God for all they have. But when her
innocent children are killed one by one, it is she
who demands that Job "curse God and die." When
he will not, she leaves him, heading to the river to
drown herself. She returns in the last scene, having
found hope and comfort in a forsythia branch
blooming at the river's edge. She has learned that
there is no justice but there is love.

Zophar

Zophar is one of the three comforters who
come to reassure J. B. in scene 9, after J. B. has lost
everything. Wearing a tattered clerical collar,
Zophar claims that "Guilt is a deceptive secret," that
man is inherently evil, and that J. B.'s suffering is
more than deserved. He represents the empty
comfort of religion, specifically of the Catholic
Church.

Mr. Zuss

Mr. Zuss, like Nickles, is an old man, an actor
who has fallen on hard times and now sells balloons
at the circus. He and Nickles are the first characters
on stage. They enter the circus tent, find a sideshow
stage, and agree to take on the characters of God
and Satan in a play-within-a-play, the biblical story
of Job. Mr. Zuss, whose name carries echoes of
"Zeus" or "Deus," will play the role of God,

wearing a white mask whose closed eyes betray no expression. He accepts a wager from Nickles/Satan: he will allow Satan to destroy everything J. B. values, and J. B. will continue to praise God. Zuss and Nickles agree that J. B. is a "perfect and upright man," that he has done nothing to deserve his destruction. Zuss believes that this relationship between God and man is proper and that for man to challenge God or seek justice from him is inappropriate.

Throughout the story of J. B./Job, Zuss and Nickles argue about J. B.'s responses. To the pompous and arrogant Zuss, it is merely fitting that J. B. should continually praise and thank him, even as J. B.'s suffering increases. When thousands are killed in an explosion and J. B. is still grateful to God, Zuss is pleased whereas Nickles is disgusted. Both men know how the story will turn out, but Nickles continually rails against what he knows will happen, whereas Zuss placidly watches the story unfold.

Themes

Hopelessness and Despair

The world *of J. B.* is a frightening world. In the beginning of the play, J. B. and his family are healthy and wealthy, happy and loving. J. B.'s children have never known suffering or deprivation; as J. B. tells Sarah, the world seems to them "New and born and fresh and wonderful." J. B. himself trusts his "luck" because it comes from God. He is safe in his knowledge that God is "just. He'll never change."

But without warning—and without cause—J. B.'s luck does change. His children are killed in particularly senseless ways: David by accident, by his own men when the war is over; Mary and Jonathan by a drunken teenaged driver; Rebecca by a teenager on drugs; Ruth in a bombing. J. B. himself is injured in an atomic blast, and his body is covered with radiation burns. There is no sense to it all, and that is the point. The world is so violent and frightening that even blameless people will be driven to despair. The surprising thing is not that Sarah eventually loses all hope, but that J. B. does not.

The hopelessness and senselessness of the world is first decried by Nickles, who speaks bitterly to Zuss, comparing the world to a "dung heap" and a "cesspool." Remembering the bombed-out cities of World War II, he says, "There never could have been so many / Suffered more for less." Throughout the play, Nickles badgers Zuss about suffering in the world and mocks humans like J. B. for thinking God cares about their suffering. The masks that Nickles and Zuss wear emphasize their relationship to human pain: Zuss's Godmask has blind eyes, but Nickles's Satanmask has open eyes, and, as Nickles says, "Those eyes *see.*" In the end, J. B. is not driven to despair, but Nickles is. Nickles comes to believe that the best thing for J. B. to do would be to commit suicide, to refuse to live in the world God has given him. For many readers, this hopelessness is the central theme of the play. It is not until the last scene that the reader has any reason to see anything more promising in the play.

Topics for Further Study

- Research the theories of communism, socialism and

Marxism. What do these groups believe about the ways societies function and should function? What do they believe about individual freedoms and responsibilities?

- The decade after World War II was a time of prosperity for many people and a time of increased poverty for others. Who profits financially from a war? Whose economic stability is threatened? Explain why this is the case.

- The use of masks for theatre and for religious practices is a tradition that reaches far back in time and all around the world. Research the ways in which masks are used in African, Native American, and other cultures to represent and to communicate with God.

- Read and research the biblical Book of Job. What is the origin of the story? When and where was it written? What questions do biblical scholars ask about the Prologue and the Epilogue? Do they agree in regard to the central idea, or question, of the book?

Justice versus Love

MacLeish himself spoke publicly and wrote about *J. B.* several times, and he was always clear as to what he believed his play was "about" (although, as the poet who created the famous lines "A poem should not mean / But be," he discussed themes with some reluctance). When he addressed the cast of a college production of the play in 1976, he stated, "The play is not a struggle between God and J. B." The central question of the play, according to the author, is "the question of the justification of the injustice of the Universe."

This theme is played out in the characters of J. B. and Sarah. From the beginning, J. B. believes that he is lucky and blessed because he has earned God's favor—that his bounty is a form of justice. When his children are taken away from him violently, one by one, he looks for reasons for his suffering. Although Nickles and Zuss (Satan and God) agree that J. B. is an innocent man who has done nothing to deserve his punishment, J. B. can think only in terms of justice, and so he concludes that he and the children must have sinned. Sarah rejects justice as the reason for their trials. In scene 8, she begs J. B. not to "betray" the children by calling them sinners: "I will not *Let you sacrifice their deaths* To make injustice justice and God good!" When J. B. refuses to listen, she leaves him.

When Sarah returns in scene 11, it is because she has learned that the world, and the humans who love in it, are reason enough to live. She explains to J. B., "You wanted justice, didn't you? *There isn't any. There's the world." She left him, she says, because "I loved you.* I couldn't help you any more. *You wanted justice and there was none—* Only love."

When MacLeish took *J. B.* to Broadway, he and the director Elia Kazan agreed that for the play to work on stage, J. B. should be the one to settle the conflict between justice and love in the end. In the acting edition, therefore, the last scene was rewritten to give J. B. most of Sarah's final lines and to expand on them. In both versions, it is clear that God does not love humans, and He does not act out of justice or injustice. He simply is. It is humans who have the capacity for love. In a world where blessings and sufferings can not be earned or deserved, people must love each other, or despair.

Style

Allusion

When a writer refers to a well-known character or story from the past, either from fiction or nonfiction, that writer is said to be using an allusion. This device works as a kind of shorthand, enabling a writer to convey a lot of information quickly and without explanation, because the reader can be assumed to bring knowledge about and responses to the things alluded to. Clearly, MacLeish's play is atleast in part a retelling of the biblical story of Job. There are several parallels between the two stories. The name "J. B." echoes the name "Job." What is more, Sarah, Nickles, and Zuss all sometimes call him by the name Job. The names of J. B.'s comforters in scene 9, Eliphaz, Zophar, and Bildad, are the names of the three comforters in the Biblical story. Although Sarah and the children are not named in the Bible, MacLeish has chosen Biblical names for each of them. The overall story, with the wager between God and Satan and the systematic destruction of all of J. B.'s possessions, echoes the story of Job. Some of the lines are direct quotations from the King James Version of the Bible.

MacLeish—and his characters Zuss and Nickles—expects that the audience is already familiar with the biblical story. When the two circus vendors arrive on the scene, Zuss indicates the stage area and comments, "That's where Job sits—at the table. *God and Satan lean above." Nickles does not ask Zuss who or what he is talking about; he knows the story and knows that the audience knows. In fact, a bit later in scene 1, Nickles summarizes the torments that Job suffered and that J. B. is about to suffer:* "God has killed his sons, his daughters, Stolen his camels, oxen, sheep, / Everything he has." Apparently, MacLeish not only does not mind that his audience knows what is going to happen to J. B.; he insists upon it.

Throughout the play, Zuss and Nickles refer to what is about to happen and occasionally speak directly to the characters to urge them to play—or not to play—their roles as written. When Rebecca's body is found, J. B. tries to utter one of the most well-known lines from the Job story. He is able to get most of the words out ("The Lord giveth... the Lord taketh away!"), but even with Zuss's urging he cannot overcome his grief and finish the line ("Blessed be the name of the Lord"). This scene works only if the audience knows the words and knows how the line is supposed to end. The point is not to tell the story, but to retell it and to comment on it, to point out that this story is reenacted over and over again.

Verse

Although he wrote plays and essays and even a screenplay, MacLeish is primarily known as a poet, and he devoted much of his life to studying poetry. *J. B.* is written entirely in verse, which was a common form for English drama in earlier centuries (many of Shakespeare's play, for example, are written in iambic pentameter verse) but extremely rare in the 1950s. When the play did well on Broadway, critics marveled that a play in verse could find an audience. *J. B.* is written in unrhymed four-stress lines without strict meter. In a conversation with college students cast for a production of the play, published as "MacLeish Speaks to the Players," the author explains that "those four syllables are accented... by the sense of the words; if you read the words to *mean,* they will take their right emphasis."

The effect of the four stresses is subtle at best; it is possible to read the dialogue without paying attention to the sound, and many readers of the text will not hear the rhythm. But when the play is performed, the four-stress line creates an undercurrent that works emotionally on the audience. For MacLeish, this undercurrent was grounded in an essential difference between poetry and prose and between myth and history. In an interview in *Horizon* magazine, he explained that while history is true at a particular place and time, stories like the story of Job are mythical, "true at any place and time: true then and therefore true forever; true forever and therefore true then." Chronological time, therefore, is less important than "always" in a drama based on myth, and "'always' exists in poetry rather than prose."

For secular readers and audiences of the early twenty-first century, drama in verse may seem as exotic as the language of the King James Bible. The language and the four-stress line serve to elevate the drama, to place it in a not-quite-familiar place and time. While the trials J. B. and his family suffer are brutally recognizable even today, the poetry of the lines achieves MacLeish's purpose: it prevents the audience from sinking into familiarity, from seeing J. B.'s story as the story of one individual man.

World War II

With the development of new technologies, World War II saw more civilian casualties than any previous war. Bombs from the air could deliver more destructive power than single bullets from a rifle, but they did not kill only soldiers, nor were they intended to. Nickles comments in scene 1 that "Millions and millions of mankind" have been "Burned, crushed, broken, mutilated," and he particularly mentions those who died because they were "Sleeping the wrong night wrong city—/ London, Dresden, Hiroshima." These three cities stand for the thousands of innocent civilians who died on both sides of the war.

Compare & Contrast

- **1940s:** Major cities in Europe and Japan suffer thousands of casualties in bombings during World War II.

  1950s: Americans live in fear of a nuclear attack.

  2001: Terrorists flying hijacked airplanes crash into the World Trade Center in New York City, into the Pentagon Building in Washington,

D.C., and into the ground at another crash site, killing or wounding over 3,000 people. It is the first time the United States has suffered a large number of civilian casualties from attackers from outside the country.

- **1940s:** CBS demonstrates color television in New York City, and WNBT, the first regularly operating television station, debuts in New York with an estimated 10,000 viewers.

  1950s: Some 29 million American homes have television—approximately one in five. Most people still get their news from newspapers.

  Today: Nearly every American home has at least one television, and most have two or more. With twenty-four-hour news channels and the ability to broadcast live from any location, television is the source most Americans turn to for news.

- **1940s:** During World War II, with the United States and the Soviet Union as wartime allies, membership in the American Communist Party reaches an all-time high of 75,000.

  1950s: Communists are hated and

feared throughout the United States. Senator Joseph McCarthy investigates alleged Communist activity within the United States and is denounced as a witchhunter. The fear of a Communist takeover of Vietnam and then the rest of Asia involves the United States in Vietnam.

Today: The American Communist Party is small, and Communism has lost much of its influence on world politics.

- **1950s:** The United States, the U.S.S.R., and Great Britain have the capability of detonating atomic bombs. Americans build bomb shelters in their homes and practice safety measures to take if a bomb is dropped on them.

Today: Although more than a dozen nations have nuclear weapons, including several "rogue nations" with unstable, unpredictable governments, Americans largely disregard the threat of nuclear attack.

London, the capital city of England, was bombed by the Nazis for fifty-eight consecutive days in 1940 and less frequently for the following six months, in the series of raids known as the Blitz. Nearly a third of the city was brought to ruins, and nearly 30,000 Londoners were killed. Dresden was one of the most beautiful cities in Germany, a center for art and culture. In February 1945, six square miles of its downtown were destroyed by Allied bombing, resulting in the deaths of between 35,000 and 135,000 people in two days. Six months later, on August 6, 1945, the first atomic bomb was dropped on the city of Hiroshima, Japan, killing almost 150,000 people.

When World War II ended in 1945, the misery did not end for people who had lived through it, particularly for people who lived in the areas that had been hardest hit by the bombing. MacLeish got the idea for *J. B.* in the late 1940s, when he visited a London suburb that had been nearly flattened by Nazi bombing. There, he met families who had been bombed in one town, moved away, and had been bombed in the new place. Many had lost relatives and friends. The senselessness of their suffering and the increasing human capacity to inflict more suffering troubled him and eventually led to *J. B.*

Cold War

Contrary to the common, nostalgic view that the 1950s was a time of unbroken happiness and prosperity, many people suffered greatly, both inside and outside the United States. World War II had just ended, and many people had lost loved ones and property. The extent of the horrors of the

Holocaust was gradually becoming known. In short, the world seemed to many people like a place where suffering and evil were not only possible but present, and without measure.

The Cold War, with the threat of nuclear annihilation, was constantly in the back of many Americans' minds. The term "Cold War" referred to the idea that the United States and the Union of Soviet Socialist Republics (USSR) were waging a political and economic battle (not a "hot" war with weapons) for influence in the world. As the two "superpowers" gained political strength, each also increased its capacity to engage in an armed conflict if necessary. The resulting arms race, in which each side eventually created enough nuclear weapons to destroy the entire planet, left people on both sides of the Cold War feeling not safer but more anxious. Even young people were exposed to the climate of fear. School children were trained to "duck and cover" in the event of an atomic bomb threat. As horrible as the destruction caused by World War II had been, the next major war threatened to leave even more misery in its wake.

Renaissance of the Verse Play

Most students are aware that Shakespeare wrote plays in iambic pentameter lines but have come to expect modern drama to be written in simple, conversational language. Some writers have felt, as the poet T. S. Eliot did in the 1930s, that the conventional language of everyday speech is not grand enough to raise important questions. Eliot decided to try to revive the verse play, producing a half dozen dramas in verse including *Murder in the Cathedral*(1935), an historical play about the assassination of the Archbishop of Canterbury in the twelfth century; and *The Cocktail Party*(1950), a combination of drawing room conversation and incantation. Audiences and critics were curious but not enamored of the form. Eliot's plays were profound and thoughtful, but often they were not good drama. *Murder in the Cathedral,* his first verse play, is generally considered his best.

In the late 1940s and early 1950s, other playwrights attempted verse drama. The British playwright Christopher Fry wrote and directed eight plays in verse. Some, including *A Sleep of Prisoners*(1951), were serious, based on religious themes; the verse supported a mystical, ponderous tone. These plays were well regarded by the critics and compared favorably with the earlier work of Eliot. Audiences much preferred Fry's comedies, including *The Lady's Not for Burning*(1948), in which the verse was a vehicle for wit, wordplay, and surprising rhythm. Fry's comedies were the first modern verse plays to be both critical and popular successes. Significantly, Fry was a playwright and director, not a poet, when he turned to this form.

MacLeish was taking a chance when he wrote *J. B.* in verse. He had written two minor radio plays in verse, and he had written hundreds of poems, but he did not have much experience as a playwright. Still, he felt as Eliot and Fry and others before him that the question he was addressing was too large and important to be expressed in prose. When he took the play to Broadway, his director Elia Kazan supervised months of revision because the play as written did not work dramatically. Everyone was surprised that the new version of the play turned out so well; it was assumed that a play based on the Bible and written in verse would draw only a small intellectual audience. Instead, *J. B.* enjoyed a long run on Broadway, won two major awards, and made a lot of money.

It was not the beginning of a trend. Verse plays continue to appear occasionally, but none has matched the success of *J. B.* Even this play, which was a staple of college theatre companies through the 1960s and 1970s, has rarely been performed since.

Critical Overview

J. B. was something of a sensation in its time, especially because of MacLeish's audacity and deftness in attempting to write verse drama for a modern audience. The play was published as a book months before it was ever performed, and so its first reviewers were readers, not members of an audience. Because MacLeish was well known as a poet, his play in verse received more critical attention in the major newspapers and magazines than it might have otherwise. The poet John Ciardi, in a review titled "Birth of a Classic," written for the *Saturday Review of Literature,* called the play "great poetry, great drama, and... great stagecraft." Other critics were more modest in their praise but were largely favorable. After its first production, at Yale University in 1958, the play was selected for the World's Fair at Brussels.

The substantially revised Broadway version of *J. B.* was widely reviewed and much discussed in bars and coffeehouses. The morning after the opening, MacLeish appeared on the *Today* show to talk about the play, and open forums were held after some of the early performances so that religious scholars could debate theology with the playwright. The play won the Pulitzer Prize for drama in 1959 (MacLeish's third Pulitzer), as well as the Tony Award for best play. It had a long run on the British stage and was translated and performed in other European countries as well. Until the early 1980s, the play was frequently performed at colleges and universities, and the book form of the play became MacLeish's best-selling work.

Criticism of the play can be divided roughly into two types: criticism (often negative) that speaks to MacLeish's religious views, reflecting on his treatment and understanding of the biblical story, and criticism (often positive) that speaks to the play as art and reflects on the author's handling of character or language or on the differences between the book and the acting edition of the play. Typical of the first type is "J. B., Wrong Answer to the Problem of Evil," written by Martin D'Arcy for *Catholic World*. D'Arcy acknowledges that *J. B.* is "good theater," but he concludes that it is bad theology because "In the solution which MacLeish offers, no reference is made to immortality nor to the Christian Cross." The conflict is summed up neatly in the title of Preston R. Gledhill's analysis in *Brigham Young University Studies*: "*J. B.*: Successful Theatre versus 'Godless' Theology." Several of these critics have quarreled with MacLeish's interpretation of the Job story, believing that in his retelling he has a duty to be completely faithful to his original source. But in a 1974 article in *Studies in Religion/Sciences Religieuses*, Elizabeth Bieman bemoans "the chasm which separates the humane vision of MacLeish's play from the conservative theology" and describes several ways in which "MacLeish opens the door to profound mystery."

Another body of criticism is willing to meet

MacLeish on his own terms. They approach the play with the expectation that the author has used the story of Job as a framework for his own work and accept that any variations he may create in his version are conscious choices, not failings to understand. As explained by Thomas E. Porter in *Myth and Modern America Drama,* MacLeish "cannot simply retell the Job story in modern terms. He has to reshape his source so that the message he finds there is translated into dramatic terms for the audience." Shannon O. Campbell, who admires MacLeish's adaptation, explicates the differences between the two versions of the story, attributing the variations to the different cultural settings, in *English Journal.* Marion Montgomery, in the journal *Modern Drama,* closely examines the fourstress line and how MacLeish varies the lines to demonstrate character and emotional states. She concludes that much of the verse is effective but that the play overall is not.

The character of J. B. is a subject for discussion. Early audiences surprised MacLeish by finding J. B. unlikable. Daniel Berrigan, in a review for *America,* comments that J. B. is not "marked by depth of character, skill and command in giving point to thought"; rather, he is "a rather simple overdrawn Main Street Type, so pale as to be invisible at noon." To Porter, however, J. B. is "the humanist hero, a responsible free agent."

What Do I Read Next?

- MacLeish draws heavily on the Book of Job, part of the Old Testament, for the basic plot and some of his characters' names. The italicized lines in the printed version of *J. B.*, spoken by Nickles, Zuss, and others, are quoted from the King James Version, first published in 1611.

- *Collected Poems, 1917-1952*(1952) was MacLeish's second Pulitzer Prize-winning book. The poems in this volume demonstrate MacLeish's range, from public to personal voice and from political to intimate themes.

- In *Songs for Eve*(1954), MacLeish draws on the biblical story of Adam and Eve's Fall and their eviction from the Garden of Eden, as he draws on the story of Job for *J. B.* Here, Eve is glad to have left Eden because the knowledge of mortality makes her feel more alive.

- The script for the play, as it was performed on Broadway in 1958, is available as *J. B.: A Play in Verse,* published by Samuel French, Inc. MacLeish and the director Elia Kazan collaborated on several substantive changes to make the play more effective dramatically and to resolve philosophical issues that Kazan felt were troublesome in MacLeish's original book.

- In the novel *The Red Badge of Courage*(1895), Stephen Crane's protagonist, Henry Fleming, sees horror and destruction as a soldier in the American Civil War and comes to wonder how God can allow such evil to exist.

Sources

Berrigan, Daniel, "Job in Suburbia," in *America,* Vol. 100, October 4, 1958, p. 13.

Bieman, Elizabeth, "Faithful to the Bible in Its Fashion: MacLeish's *J. B.,*" in *Studies in Religion/Sciences Religieuses,* Vol. 4, 1974, pp. 25, 27.

Calhoun, Richard, "Archibald MacLeish's *J. B.:* Religious Humanism in the 80s," in *The Proceedings of the Archibald MacLeish Symposium May 7-8, 1982,* edited by Bernard A.

Drabeck, Helen E. Ellis, and Seymour Rudin, University Press of America, 1988, pp. 79-80.

Campbell, Shannon O., *"The Book of Job* and MacLeish's *J. B.:* A Cultural Comparison," in *English Journal,* Vol. 61, May 1972, pp. 653-57.

Ciardi, John, "Birth of a Classic," in *Saturday Review of Literature,* Vol. 41, March 8, 1958, p. 48.

D'Arcy, Martin, "J. *B.,* Wrong Answer to the Problem of Evil," in *Catholic World,* Vol. 190, November 1959, p. 82.

Gledhill, Preston R., *"J. B.:* Successful Theatre versus 'Godless' Theology," in *Brigham Young University Studies,* Vol. 3, December 1961, pp. 9-14.

Kahn, Sy, "The Games God Plays with Man: A Discussion of *J. B.,*" in *The Fifties: Fiction, Poetry,*

Drama, edited by Warren French, Everett/Edwards, 1970, pp. 250, 255.

MacLeish, Archibald, Foreword to *J. B.,* Samuel French, 1958, p. 6.

_____, "MacLeish Speaks to the Players," in *Pembroke Magazine,* Vol. 7, 1976, pp. 80, 82, 83.

_____, "On Being a Poet in the Theatre," in *Horizon,* Vol. 12, January 1960, p. 50.

Montgomery, Marion, "On First Looking into Archibald MacLeish's Play in Verse, *J. B.,*" in *Modern Drama,* Vol. 2, December 1959, pp. 231-42.

Porter, Thomas E., *Myth and Modern American Drama,* Wayne State University Press, 1969, pp. 82, 96.

Roston, Murray, *Biblical Drama in England: From the Middle Ages to the Present Day,* Northwestern University Press, 1968, p. 309.

Trudeau, Gary, *Doonesbury,* Universal Press Syndicate, October 5, 2001.

Further Reading

Donaldson, Scott, in collaboration with R. H. Winnick, *Archibald MacLeish: An American Life,* Houghton Mifflin, 1992.

> In this definitive biography of MacLeish, the discussion of J. *B.* presents MacLeish's reasons for writing the play and describes his writing and revising process as he moved from written script to performance.

Drabeck, Bernard A., and Helen E. Ellis, eds., *Archibald MacLeish: Reflections,* University of Massachusetts Press, 1986.

> Arranged in a question-and-answer format, this book was pieced together from several interviews MacLeish granted during the last years of his life. MacLeish considered this book the autobiography of his professional life. His discussion of *J. B.* focuses on the differences between the published and the performed versions of the play.

Ellis, Helen E., Bernard A. Drabeck, and Margaret E. C. Howland, *Archibald MacLeish: A Selectively Annotated Bibliography,* Scarecrow Press, 1995.

With more than twenty-three hundred entries and two indices, this book is an excellent starting-place for locating books, articles, and reviews by and about the author. The book also includes a brief biography and a chronology of significant dates in MacLeish's life.

Falk, Signi Lenea, *Archibald MacLeish,* Twayne, 1965.

In an analysis of the first half century of MacLeish's career, Falk demonstrates how MacLeish's poetry grew out of and then away from the poetry of other important modern poets and how all of his writing came to demonstrate his convictions about a writer's responsibilities to address the political and social world. The book includes a thirteen-page close reading of *J. B.*

Gassner, John, *Theatre at the Crossroads: Plays and Playwrights of the Mid-Century American Stage,* Holt, Rinehard and Winston, 1960.

After an analysis that leads toward generalities about the plays produced in New York from the end of World War II through the 1950s, Gassner examines dozens of individual plays. His analysis of *J. B.* focuses on the differences between the Yale and the Broadway productions.